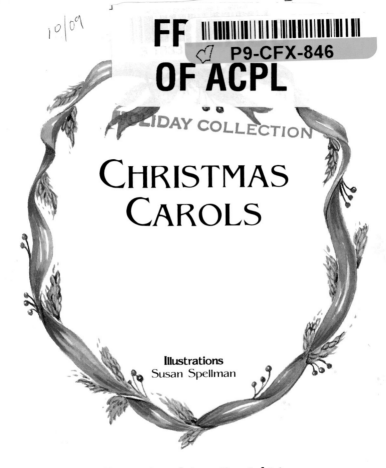

HOLIDAY COLLECTION

CHRISTMAS CAROLS

Illustrations
Susan Spellman

Publications International, Ltd.

Deck the halls with boughs of
   holly!
   Fa la la la la la la la la.
'Tis the season to be jolly,
   Fa la la la la la la la la.
Don we now our gay apparel,
   Fa la la la la la la la la.
Troll the ancient Yule-tide carol,
   Fa la la la la la la la la.

Dashing through the snow,
  In a one-horse open sleigh,
O'er the fields we go,
  Laughing all the way.

Bells on bob-tail ring,
  Making spirits bright,
What fun it is to ride and sing
  A sleighing song tonight!

Jingle bells! Jingle bells!
  Jingle all the way!
Oh, what fun it is to ride
  In a one-horse open sleigh!

Jolly old Saint Nicholas,
  Lean your ear this way!
Don't you tell a single soul
  What I'm going to say;
Christmas Eve is coming soon;
  Now you dear old man,
Whisper what you'll bring to me;
  Tell me if you can.

O Christmas tree! O Christmas tree!
  Your leaves are faithful ever!
O Christmas tree! O Christmas tree!
  Your leaves are faithful ever!

Not only green when summer glows,
  But in the winter when it snows,
O Christmas tree! O Christmas tree!
  Your leaves are faithful ever.

We wish you a Merry Christmas,
  We wish you a Merry Christmas,
We wish you a Merry Christmas,
  And a happy New Year.

Good tidings we bring
  To you and your kin.
We wish you a Merry Christmas,
  And a happy New Year.

Christmas is coming!
    The geese are getting fat!
Please to put a penny
    in an old man's hat,
Please to put a penny
    in an old man's hat.
If you have no penny,
    a ha'penny will do,
If you have no ha'penny,
    a farthing will do,
If you have no farthing,
    then God bless you.

Silent night, holy night,
   All is calm, all is bright
Round yon virgin mother and
      child,
   Holy infant so tender and mild.
Sleep in heavenly peace,
   Sleep in heavenly peace.

Silent night, holy night,
   Shepherds quake at the sight,
Glories stream from heaven
      afar,
   Heavenly hosts sing alleluia,
Christ the Savior is born!
   Christ the Savior is born!

The first Noël the angels did say,
  Was to certain poor shepherds
    in fields as they lay;
In fields where they lay keeping
    their sheep,
  On a cold winter's night that
    was so deep.

Noël, Noël, Noël, Noël,
  Born is the King of Israel!

Joy to the world!
  The Lord has come;
    Let earth receive her King.
Let every heart
      prepare Him room,
And heaven and nature sing,
  And heaven and nature sing,
And heaven, and heaven and
      nature sing.